CANBY PUBLIC LIBRARY
292 N. HOLLY
CANBY, OR 97013

D0599211

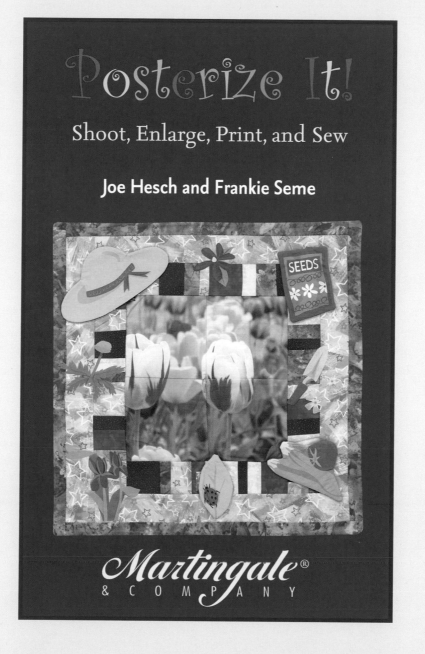

Posterize It!

Shoot, Enlarge, Print, and Sew

Joe Hesch and Frankie Seme

Martingale®
& COMPANY

DONATED
MATERIAL

Posterize It! Shoot, Enlarge, Print, and Sew
© 2007 by Joe Hesch and Frankie Seme

That Patchwork Place® is an imprint of Martingale & Company®.

Martingale & Company
20205 144th Ave. NE
Woodinville, WA 98072-8478
www.martingale-pub.com

No part of this product may be reproduced in any form, unless otherwise stated, in which case reproduction is limited to the use of the purchaser. The written instructions, photographs, designs, projects, and patterns are intended for the personal, noncommercial use of the retail purchaser and are under federal copyright laws; they are not to be reproduced by any electronic, mechanical, or other means, including informational storage or retrieval systems, for commercial use. Permission is granted to photocopy patterns for the personal use of the retail purchaser. Attention teachers: Martingale & Company encourages you to use this book for teaching, subject to the restrictions stated above.

The information in this book is presented in good faith, but no warranty is given nor results guaranteed. Since Martingale & Company has no control over choice of materials or procedures, the company assumes no responsibility for the use of this information.

Printed in China
12 11 10 09 08 07   8 7 6 5 4 3 2 1

Library of Congress Cataloging-in-Publication Data
Library of Congress Control Number: 2007000268

ISBN: 978-1-56477-745-4

CREDITS

President & CEO: Tom Wierzbicki
Publisher: Jane Hamada
Editorial Director: Mary V. Green
Managing Editor: Tina Cook
Developmental Editor:
     Karen Costello Soltys
Technical Editor: Ellen Pahl
Copy Editor: Melissa Bryan
Design Director: Stan Green
Illustrator: Robin Strobel
Cover & Text Designer: Stan Green
Photographer: Brent Kane

MISSION STATEMENT

Dedicated to providing quality products and service to inspire creativity.

Contents

Seascape, a blend of photos and fabrics, 26" x 27"

Introduction

With this book, we're introducing a new word to the English language. *Posterize*, according to us, means "to create a print using 8½" x 11" printable fabric sheets, usually piecing them together to make a larger, poster-sized print." You can call it whatever you wish, but a photo printed "super sized" onto fabric really makes a statement. It is easier to do than you may think, and you probably have all the equipment you need right at home. Now, combine photo printing onto fabric with your love for sewing, and you can create beautiful keepsakes that will be cherished for generations. It's fun, it's easy, and we'll show you how!

In this book, you'll learn everything you need to create beautiful wall hangings and quilts as well as any other projects that you can dream up. We'll teach you the tips and tricks of fabric printing plus how to get the best-quality prints using the equipment you already have. We give you step-by-step instructions for five projects, beginning with one quick-and-easy project for sewers of any level. Pick your favorite photo, frame it with a coordinating fabric, and sew it all together. This is fun, unique, and can only be created with your personal touch.

Feathered Nostalgia by Ellen Pahl, 30" x 31"

Wedding Kaleidoscope, created using Kaleidoscope Kreator II software, 33" x 33"

Printable Fabric Sheets— The Foundation of Your Project

A printable fabric sheet is simply a piece of fabric treated with an ink fixative (for washability) and backed with a sheet of paper or plastic. The backing gives the fabric the necessary rigidity to feed through a printer. These sheets, plus the use of an inkjet printer, provide the basis for the projects in this book. Printable fabric sheets can be made at home or purchased. It's up to you. We'll cover both options.

There are many kinds of printable fabric sheets available commercially. At the time of this writing, there are least eight different types of silk and more than 20 different types of cotton, with new choices on the market every year. There are iron-on fabrics (which can be ironed after printing), heavy denims, and wispy silk chiffons, among others. There are colorful fabrics, white fabrics, and fabrics of almost any size. Be sure to check "Resources" on page 63 if you need help locating the supplies we discuss.

Fabric Type

People often ask us, "What types of fabric sheets are best?" We always answer, "That depends . . ." When you are making a traditional wall hanging, a nice cotton poplin does the trick. If you are creating something that you might be snuggling in, we suggest a soft cotton lawn. If you are making a wall hanging with an outdoorsy theme, perhaps a denim or twill would be an appropriate match. Vintage images gain added character when printed on linen, and baby quilts will be soft and snuggly when images are printed on silk. In this book, we'll focus only on our favorites for poster-sized projects.

Cotton

Cotton is the standard fabric for most projects; it results in high-quality photos and has a nice feel. Good brands to use are Color Textiles, Printed Treasures, Electric Quilt, and Vintage Workshop. We prefer poplin for the best print quality because it has a tight weave and is the closest match that we can find to actual photo paper. Cotton lawn is a nice alternative for "snuggly" quilts because it has a looser weave and is a bit softer. Electric Quilt makes a satin-finish cotton that has a very pleasing feel to it. It's fabulous for pillows. The bright white cottons yield the brightest, sharpest colors.

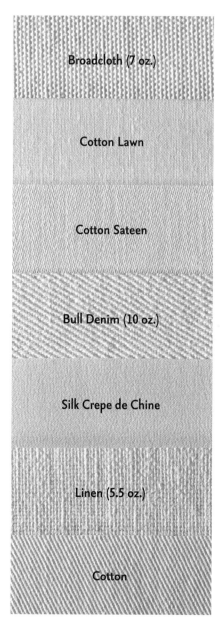

Broadcloth (7 oz.)

Cotton Lawn

Cotton Sateen

Bull Denim (10 oz.)

Silk Crepe de Chine

Linen (5.5 oz.)

Cotton

Frankie's Girls, 36" x 41"

Silk

Printable silk has a soft, refined feel that makes it an excellent choice for baby quilts and, in some instances, pillows. If you want to use silk for a poster, use the heaviest weight you can find. Silk satin tends to fray and stretch on the bias more readily than cotton or denim. This, and the fact that it is slippery, makes silk a little more difficult when you want to line up printed poster panels. It's a superb fabric, though, and if you follow our guidelines, you should be able to create a nice project.

Silk twill has a different weave than satin and works really well for pillows. Our favorite supplier of silk is Color Textiles, and their technical-support staff is very helpful and generous with advice on which type of silk to use for a specific project. We love silk and encourage you to give it a try—if not for a larger poster quilt, at least on a small project such as "The Patient Kitty" on page 40.

Denim

Denim is a heavier woven cotton that is sturdy, easy to work with, and creates a unique texture for photos. It is an excellent choice for a Western theme or outdoor-type photos. It does require some special care when being pieced together, however, because you'll have more difficulty seeing where the edges of the image line up on denim as opposed to poplin or plain cotton. Probably the most desirable trait of denim is its ability to hang flat without quilting. Softer fabrics such as cotton lawn, silk, or even poplin need support to keep the fabric stable when hanging. However, denim is thick enough and sturdy enough to hang flat, similar to canvas, making it a good choice for wall hangings.

Linen

Linen has a looser weave than cotton lawn, making it the perfect choice for a number of projects. We like it for vintage photo work, because it replicates that feed-sack look of the 1930s. It also works great for pillows and some clothing applications; you can add machine-embroidery designs to it just as easily as with other fabrics. Vintage Workshop and Color Textiles both carry linen of good quality. (See "Resources" on page 63.)

Commercially Prepared Printable Fabric Sheets

From our experience, all manufacturers are offering good-quality products with minimal difference in price. New products are continually being created, so check quilt shops and vendors at shows for the newest products.

We find that the biggest differences in printable fabric sheets are the hand of the fabric and the ability to retain color after washing. It's very important to follow the manufacturer's washing and care instructions. Make no mistake, printable fabric sheets rarely hold up like commercially prepared fabric—that is, any fabric that is dyed at a factory. All fabrics are subject to abrasion and fading, but printable fabrics are not as durable. Treat them as you would any delicate fabric.

Don't let that discourage you, however. Projects such as wall hangings, pillows, and decorative quilts are rarely used in a manner that soils them. Think about heirloom quilts, or artwork hanging on the wall. Would you throw them in the washing machine? Probably not. But if needed, many of the fabrics listed in the chart below stand up nicely to several hand washings using quilt soap. When properly cared for, these projects will easily last for generations.

Commercially Available Printable Fabric Sheets

BRAND	PRODUCTS
COLOR TEXTILES	Many different kinds of silks and cottons in cut-sheet sizes as well as yardage on rolls in widths designed to go through printers. Nice washability, and fabric is pretreated with a good paper backing. We really like their rolls of silk fabric. Fabrics are available online and through many quilt stores and sewing-machine dealers.
JUNE TAILOR	Brilliantly white fabric sheets that produce excellent photo quality and hang nicely because of their stiffness. Some people have complained of images fading over time, but we have not experienced this.
VINTAGE WORKSHOP	Good-quality cotton and linen fabric sheets. They sell fabric sampler kits that include the fabrics plus a CD with vintage images for printing. We especially like their linen fabric.
ELECTRIC QUILT	Regular cotton, cotton lawn, and cotton satin. The fabrics come in bright colors and have a nice plastic backing. All have excellent washability and are top-rate products. The cotton satin feels wonderful and produces an image of very high quality.
PRINTED TREASURES	A consistently good-quality cotton that has set the standard for reliability and washability. The fabric may pill a bit more than other brands over time, but it washes nicely and has a very soft hand.

Making Your Own Fabric Sheets

Making your own printable fabric sheets requires some time and preparation, but can be done at about half the cost of buying the commercial brands. You'll need 100%-cotton fabric or any other natural fabric such as linen or silk. For backing, you'll need either freezer paper or full-sheet adhesive labels that are available at office-supply stores. You'll also need an ink fixative, such as Bubble Jet Set 2000, to make the fabric colorfast. (See "Resources" on page 63, or check your local quilt shop.)

We like to make our own sheets when we are searching for "just the right fabric." Although you can find a nice variety of commercially prepared fabric sheets, there are times when you need a special fabric that you just can't locate on the retail market. For instance, we have repaired antique quilts that have been damaged by wear, fire, rips, stains, or moths. The damaged fabric was no longer available, of course, so we simply scanned a representative portion of the quilt and then printed new yardage on fabric sheets we made ourselves. Antique fabric often has a unique weave or hand, and sometimes we do a fair amount of searching through our stash or at the fabric store to find a good match. Then we simply follow the instructions below to make our own printable fabric sheets. (You can scan and print antique fabrics, but be aware that current fabrics are copyright protected.)

Note: When making your own fabric sheets, be sure to use a commercial rinse, such as Bubble Jet Rinse, after printing. We suggest purchasing the rinse when you purchase the fixative.

Supplies

Fabric: 100% cotton, linen, or silk
Ink fixative, such as Bubble Jet Set 2000
Plastic dishpan or other container
Iron
Firm, smooth ironing surface, such as a cloth-covered table
    or piece of shelving
Scissors or rotary cutter
Ruler
Cutting mat
Freezer paper or full-sheet adhesive labels
Lint brush
Bubble Jet Rinse (See page 11)

Detail of **Summer's Riches** by Ellen Pahl, 31" x 48"

Preparing Fabric

1. Pretreat the fabric with the ink fixative, following the manufacturer's directions for pretreating and drying the fabric. It's a simple process, and you can even reuse the fixative (simply pour the excess back in the bottle).

2. Iron the fabric to remove wrinkles. Use a dry iron on the cotton setting for best results.

3. Cut a 9" x 11½" piece of ironed fabric. By cutting the fabric slightly larger than the finished 8½" x 11" sheet, you'll greatly reduce the possibility of getting adhesive or wax on your iron and ironing surface. You'll trim the fabric to fit the backing later.

4. Cut an 8½" x 11" piece of freezer paper. (If using an adhesive label, see "Using Adhesive Sheets" on page 12.) Place the treated fabric face down on the ironing surface. Center the freezer paper, shiny side down, over the fabric. Iron the freezer paper until it bonds to the fabric. Start in the center and iron out to the edge, making sure the corners and sides are completely bonded. Turn the sheet over and briefly iron the fabric side, removing any remaining wrinkles.

DON'T SCORCH

When bonding the freezer paper to the fabric, do most of the ironing on the freezer-paper side to reduce the possibility of scorching the fabric.

5. Brush the fabric with a lint brush to remove any lint just before you print. It's best to use the fabric sheets immediately after making them.

STORING FABRIC SHEETS

If you won't be using the prepared fabric sheets right away, make sure the sheets are flat when you store them. We store ours in a plastic bag and place something heavy on top, such as a phone book. This keeps them from curling up or separating.

USING ADHESIVE SHEETS

We have found that using full-sheet adhesive labels instead of freezer paper works very well. The label sheets bond a little better to the fabric than freezer paper does. Simply stick them to the fabric and trim the fabric to the size of the label. Here are some pointers for using adhesive labels.

- Use only full-sheet adhesive labels (one label per sheet) for creating fabric sheets. Don't use smaller labels such as address labels because they may peel off inside the printer. Trust us . . . we tried it, and it wasn't pretty!
- Be sure that the weave of the fabric is square on the label for each sheet. If it isn't, your sheets won't match and you may end up printing on the bias.

Emily Swimming, 43" x 34"

Printers and Ink

In this section we cover what to look for in printers and answer many of the questions we get in our seminars. To begin, printable fabric sheets are designed primarily for inkjet printers, not laser printers. How do you know if your printer is an inkjet or a laser? Look at the ink/toner that you use. If you replace toner that is in a large cartridge and it gets your hands dirty, you probably have a laser printer. If your printer uses small cartridges that cost a lot of money, chances are you have an inkjet!

All joking aside, inkjet printers are what most households have today. They come in the form of traditional single-function printers, photo printers, and the popular all-in-one printer/scanner/fax machine. We like the all-in-one models because of their versatility and because you can create many projects without the use of a computer. Let's take a look at brands, features, and inks.

Printer Brands

You have a choice of many printer brands on the market. We prefer the Hewlett-Packard (HP) and Epson models, primarily because of the durability of the ink (providing greater washability), ease of use, and quality of the print. HP is the most prevalent in the United States and for that reason, we use them for examples in this book.

Epson clearly provides the best washability of all inkjet printers because it has pigment-based ink, meaning that it stays in the fabric much better than dye-based ink. Epson is the only manufacturer we know of that has pigment-based ink in home inkjet printers. At the time of this writing, we have heard that HP is coming out with a pigment-based ink, but we have not had a chance to test it yet. In our opinion, all other printers on the market are close runners-up to HP and Epson.

It is important to note that newer printers (those less than two years old) will have the best ink formulations and give you the best print quality. With that said, any inkjet printer will actually work for printing on fabric, so don't feel that you need to rush out and buy a new one.

Detail of **How Tall Are You?** 20" x 46"

Printer Features and Types

Can your printer make a poster? How do you know? With the myriad printers on the market today, it can become confusing. First, open the Properties, Preferences, or Settings window for your printer. Then look under the Finishing, Features, or Page Layout tab; here you will see the poster printing option, if available. This option allows you to create an enlarged copy of your original in sections to assemble into a poster. If your printer does not have this feature, there is software that can do it for you. See "Four Ways to Posterize a Photo" on page 23.

Microsoft product screen shot reprinted with permission from Microsoft Corporation.

Most printers will print 8½" x 11" sheets, but if you have an HP 8750 or an Epson R2400 printer, you will be able to print 13" x 19" sheets.

There are three major types of home inkjet printers: all-in-one printers, photo printers, and single-function printers.

All-in-One Printers

Our top choice in printers is the all-in-one model. These printers can scan, copy, and print photos, as well as send and receive faxes. They offer excellent versatility and print quality, at a cost ranging from $100 to $300. Some of these printers allow you to make posters without even using a computer, but certain models—those that do not have the poster function available as part of the copying options—can only print a poster if the printer is also connected to a computer. If this factor is important to you, be sure to check the printer's features before you buy.

All-in-one photo printer

Another advantage of these printers is the scanner. A scanner is essentially a specialized digital camera that takes pictures from a very close distance. You can place items on the scanner and make a collage, or three-dimensional image, as we did for "Remembering Grandma Bredeson" on page 44. Scanners have a limited "depth of field," meaning the distance from the glass bed at which a scanner can still reproduce an image. This distance is typically about 1" to 2" but varies depending on the scanner. We have found that most Epson scanners have a fairly short depth of field (less than 1") and the HPs have about a 2" to 3" depth of field.

Photo Printers

Photo printers are single-function printers designed expressly for printing photos. This type of printer would be our second choice. Photo printers can normally accept any type of digital camera memory chips/sticks and can print pictures without a computer attached. They are more expensive ($200 and up) than other printers, but they also yield the best photo quality. Some all-in-one printers are also photo printers.

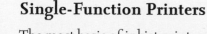

Photo printer

Single-Function Printers

The most basic of inkjet printers is the single-function printer. These models can cost as little as $49 and do a good job. They account for the vast majority of printers in the home. They print only from a computer and do nothing else, which makes them our third choice. Many of the lower-cost printers may not have the poster printing capability, so be sure to check before you buy.

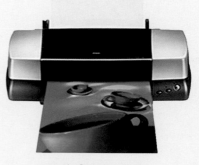

Single-function printer

Ink

We are often asked, "Do I have to use my photo cartridge?" "What inks are best?" "Can I use refills?" All these are good questions, and here are the answers.

In our experience, it is not necessary to use photo cartridges, but they will yield slightly better results. You will clearly notice a difference when printing on photo paper, but remember that fabric is a coarser, less refined medium that can't always take advantage of the finer qualities of a photo cartridge. Try it out to see what you think. We have found very little difference on fabric.

Not all printer ink is the same. In the section on printers, we mentioned the pigment-based inks used by Epson. Those pigments really hang on to the fabric and make for the best washability. Look for Epson printers that use the DuraBrite, UltraBrite, or UltraChrome inks. Dye-based inks, used by all other inkjet manufacturers, are better suited to abrasion but don't do as well in wash tests. From our experience, HP ink has proven to be the best all-around ink for color and print quality, but Epson pigment-based inks are clearly the best for washability.

Refills and remanufactured inks are a cost-saving alternative these days. Can you use them for your poster quilts? Yes, you can, but we recommend using the manufacturer's original ink cartridges for best results. When you are printing pictures or printing on fabric, you may not get the same washability or print quality with remanufactured or refilled cartridges as you do with the manufacturer's original equipment.

Young Romance, 14" x 16"

Designing a Poster Quilt

Your imagination is the only limitation to what you can do when designing quilts using images printed onto fabric. It's really fun to combine new technology with old to create something wonderful using the best of both worlds.

Choosing a Photo

Choosing just the right photo makes a big difference in the look of your finished project. We try to avoid very dark photos—they simply don't look as nice when printed. Simple images and bright colors in your photo work best.

If you are working with digital photos (from your digital camera or a CD) be sure you have a photo with a reasonable file size. What is reasonable? Well, since you'll be enlarging your photo dramatically, you'll benefit from the highest resolution or largest file size that's available to you. For the smallest poster of four panels set 2 x 2, we start with nothing less than a 1-megabyte (1 MB) file. Anything less will not look very good when enlarged. To find out how big the file is, look in your computer and the file size may be listed right next to the file. If not, you can right-click on the file icon, and then click on Properties. Some digital cameras will give you the file size as well.

If you are scanning a paper photo to be enlarged, use a scan setting of 600 dpi (dots per inch) to be sure you get enough detail. Of course, if you are starting out with a photo that is very small (wallet size), you may have to scan at an even higher resolution. Before printing onto fabric, always print a test on plain paper on the Draft or Fast setting to judge how the finished project will look.

Determine the Layout

Once you have chosen a photo, determine the orientation of the photo and the layout of your quilt. It can be as simple as an enlargement printed on one fabric sheet and surrounded by a border, or as complex as enlarging and printing a photo onto 25 fabric sheets and sewing them together with or without sashing. Read on to design a unique quilt perfectly suited for your chosen image.

Landscape or Portrait

When doing a trial printout, test your print in both Landscape and Portrait layout. Selecting the option labeled Landscape will print your image horizontally,

Detail of **Hydrangeas in the Summer,** 23" x 31"

while selecting Portrait will print it vertically. You will achieve dramatically different results, and your image will split in different places even when choosing the same number of panels or tiles. (Some computers use the term *tiling* or *multi-page* when referring to panels.) Doing a test print on paper will help you conserve your fabric and will allow you to alter where your photo splits based on the number of panels you chose.

Choose the Number of Panels

Two, four, six, eight . . . or more? It all depends on the size you want and what you are trying to do. More often than not, the number of panels or tiles you choose is dictated by the photo. The largest we have printed is a poster made up of 25 panels set 5 x 5. When you decide to print a poster, examine your photo to see if it will naturally split up into a certain number of panels.

In typical photographs, the subject is often centered. Splitting the print into pieces for a poster can lead to the seams falling right in the middle of the subject's face. We call this the "bull's-eye effect." It may be better to choose a picture like the one below left. If your heart is set on a specific picture, consider splitting it into a different number of panels so seam lines do not fall on critical areas. Fine facial features, text, and small details are hard to match up when you are sewing. It is easier to match up solid colors or aggregate features such as leaves or water. Other irregular and unimportant parts of the picture are usually not a problem to split and sew back together.

Graduation, 3 x 3 with 1-page borders, 72" x 92"

Two subjects, not centered, may be easier to split into panels.

This subject is centered, creating the "bull's-eye effect."

Unfortunately, there is very little you can do to control exactly where the printer will split a picture. That is programmed into the software and we have not found a good way around the built-in settings. Typically, we simply alter the number of panels to control where the split occurs, or we crop the photo to alter its proportion. You can determine this with test printouts on paper before you print on fabric.

Windowpane Sashing

If you'd like to create a windowpane quilt such as those shown at right, you can use sashing to sew your panels back together after printing. This is a fun way to create the illusion of looking out a window, and it is a great way to cover misaligned images along the seams. A photograph with an outdoor setting or theme is ideal for the windowpane technique. Any image that you might see outside of a window would be a good choice.

You will need a print that works well divided into a 2 x 3 or 3 x 3 layout for best results. You can use more panels than that, but you'll begin to lose the realistic windowpane simulation. As always, do a test print on paper to determine where the seams will fall.

Here's another advantage of windowpane sashing: if you can't seem to get the panels to match up correctly when you're sewing them together, simply add sashing and it won't be as noticeable.

Julia Fishing, 33" x 27"

Benjamin's Day with Dad, 45" x 35"

Choose Your Frames or Finishing Style

After you piece together your printed image, there are many different ways to finish or frame your photograph when making it into a quilt or wall hanging. Each of the projects included in this book has a different type of frame or finishing style. Often your choice depends on the theme of the photo you have selected. This section highlights some of the different frames and finishes, why you might choose them, and where they might work best. There are lots of fun choices for finishing your quilt or wall hanging. Choose the one that works best for you and your image, and don't be afraid to combine methods.

Basic Borders

If you have a traditional look in mind for your quilt, basic borders may be your best choice. If you use one border, it's like putting a picture frame around your favorite photograph. See "Remembering Grandma Bredeson" on page 44 for an example. If you add more than one border, it's somewhat like using a mat around a print or photograph.

Anna Cowgirl, *12" x 15" without lace*

Appliqué

Another option after you have printed or pieced together your image is to use appliqué techniques for finishing. This creates a unique look and opens up many avenues for experimentation. Here are some examples of what you can do.

The image as the appliqué. In the quilt at right, the printed image was pieced together and then cut into a circular shape before being appliquéd to the background fabric. This gave the quilt the appearance of looking through an underwater porthole.

Fussy-cut appliqué, or broderie perse. In "Sunflower Girl," sunflower appliqués add a wonderful three-dimensional look to the photo image. The flowers emphasize the theme of a warm summer day and accent this bright and sunny photograph. In this case, we cut the sunflower fabric into individual clusters of flowers and appliquéd them onto the printed image, rather than cutting the printed image. The appliquéd flowers soften the traditional borders, as do the rounded corners. Appliqué techniques provide you with some wonderful, fun, and creative looks for framing or finishing!

Emily Swimming, 43" x 34"

Sunflower Girl, 67" x 52"

Posterizing (Printing) Your Photo

Once you've chosen a photo and made decisions about the design of your project, it's time to prepare the photo and do test printing on paper. Then you'll be ready to posterize—that is, print your photo at poster size—onto fabric.

Prepping the Photo

To prepare your photo for printing, you may first want to do some color correction, cropping, red-eye removal, or any number of special effects using photo-editing software. Use a program you are comfortable with or check your print driver. In many cases, especially with photo printers, your print driver will have the necessary software to help you correct photos.

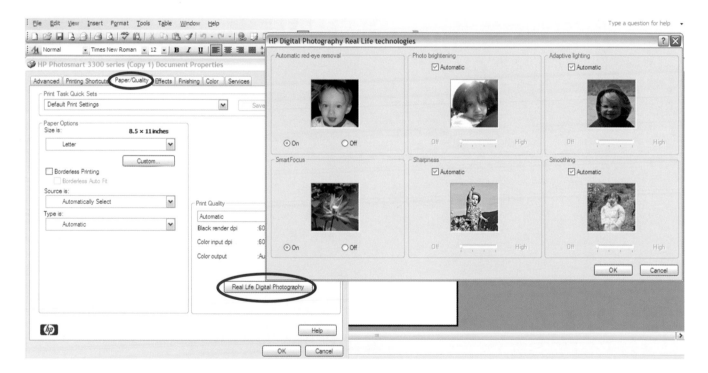

Before printing, strive for the cleanest and best representation of the photograph you intend to posterize. Photos often look a bit different when they are enlarged to this size, so always be sure to do a test print on plain paper first.

Microsoft product screen shot reprinted with permission from Microsoft Corporation.

Four Ways to Posterize a Photo

There are basically four ways to posterize or print your photo onto fabric. Read on to see which is the best option for you.

Using Software and a Computer

Since many software programs are available for printing photos, we cannot give you step-by-step instructions in this book for each one, but we can make a recommendation. Poster 7 is a nice program available online that makes creating a poster quite simple. This program is available for a free trial and you can print up to 10 images before you are required to pay the registration fee. (The fee is quite reasonable.) See "Resources" on page 63 for additional information. Most other programs fall into the category of desktop-publishing programs; a search on the Internet will uncover a number of options.

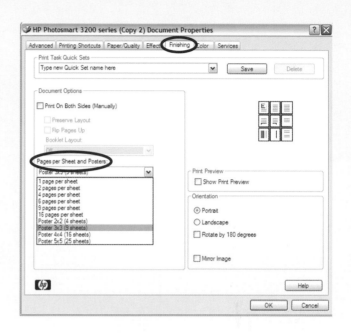

Using the Print Driver

Using the print driver is the easiest and most economical method, since you are basically printing a single photo in a poster size. This is our favorite technique and is the one we most commonly use. It's also an option that almost everyone has at his or her disposal right now, but simply may not know it. Inkjet printers have long been designed to include the poster-printing capability—all you need to know is where to look. Simply select Print from within any software program and choose Properties or Preferences from the print driver. Typically, the poster function will be under the Finishing or Page Layout tab. At right are two examples, one showing an HP screen and one from an Epson printer. Since there are so many printer models to choose from, we can't cover them all, but this information should help lead you where you need to go.

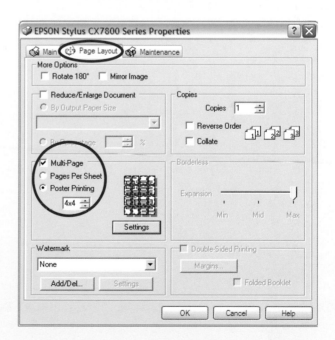

Microsoft product screen shots reprinted with permission from Microsoft Corporation.

Using the Copy Function of an All-in-One Printer

If you're not particularly interested in computers, you may find this section interesting. You also may be surprised to know that many of the projects in this book have been completed with no computer at all! Many of the all-in-one copier/scanner/printer machines have the poster capability built into the copier. Essentially, you use the machine as a stand-alone copier completely independent from the computer. In fact, you don't even need to own a computer if you have one of these printers.

We can't cover all the models, but the illustration below from an HP 2610 shows how easy it is to use the copier to enlarge a photo to a poster. Simply follow the three easy steps and copy a photo or three-dimensional collage into a poster up to 4 x 4 (16 sheets of fabric). Be sure to refer to the owner's manual for your copier or, if you don't have the manual, look within the Reduce/ Enlarge option on the copier—that's where your poster function will most likely be listed.

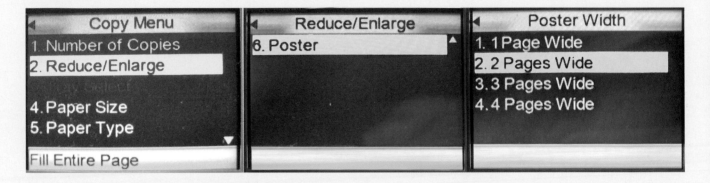

Cutting the Photo Apart

Physically cutting apart your photo and enlarging it has a few advantages. First, you can control exactly where the splits in the photo will occur. Second, you can control exactly how many pieces you will be using; you're not limited to the choices your printer provides. To create a poster in this manner, you will need a scanner or all-in-one printer.

1. Make a copy of your original photo. Cut the copy into the number of sections you prefer. They do not necessarily have to be equal in size, but they will need to be enlarged by the same amount.

2. You will need to do some trial printing using the Reduce/Enlarge function to determine the enlargement percentage that will work best. Each section of the photo needs to be copied using exactly the same enlargement setting. We recommend you enlarge the pieces by using a *percentage* rather than an image size (such as Fit to Page). Enlarging by a percentage ensures that all your pieces are proportionate to each other and fit well together. If you choose Fit to Page, the copier will take each piece and enlarge it to fit your 8½" x 11" fabric sheet regardless of the size of the original piece; you will end up with proportionately dissimilar sections.

One disadvantage to this method is that it is a little trickier to use a windowpane sashing unless you are *very* careful of how you cut up your image. If using a windowpane sashing, you would need to cut each piece to the same dimensions. The other disadvantage is that this method requires a bit more trial and error to determine the exact percentage for enlargement. It's not as simple as using the poster function. It is critical to do a test print on paper first to see how your project will look.

Test Printing on Paper

Put some plain paper in your printer and do some experimentation with a photo from a digital camera or one you have stored in your computer. With your printer in the poster mode, select different sizes, change from portrait to landscape, use different photos, and so on. This is the best way to develop your skills and become confident. Remember that printers are no more complicated than sewing machines, and you've mastered those! Just take some time, play a little, and have fun. You will be amazed at what you learn about the capabilities of your printer.

We can't say this enough—always do a test print of any photo before printing on fabric. Then lay all the pieces on the floor or a table, and look at your print to make sure it looks the way you want it to. This will also allow you to check the color, the resolution, the positioning, and the breaks. There may be times when you want to do some cropping and make other adjustments to modify the breaks or the way the image is printed on the page. Remember, paper is cheap, but the fabric sheets are not.

Printing

You've now learned about the various ways to enlarge your photo to new dimensions. Once you are satisfied with your test print on paper, you are ready to print on fabric. Read through this section for instructions and tips that will ensure that your printed fabric panels are of outstanding quality.

1. First, adjust the settings to obtain the best print quality. Always . . . always . . . *always* set your print quality to Best and your paper type to Plain. The screen shot below shows how we made those selections on an HP printer. These options can be found in your print driver.

2. In your print driver, go to the color window. Increase your color saturation a small amount as shown. With these settings, you will achieve great results.

3. Remove any paper from the tray and load one fabric sheet at a time into your printer so that the printer won't pick up two at once. The paper side of the fabric sheet should be facing up or down, depending on your printer. If you're unsure, mark an X on a piece of paper and do a test print to see which way to load the fabric sheet.

4. Print your images. You can remove each sheet as it comes out of the printer, but it's also OK if the sheets pile up as they come out.

5. Let the ink dry (it only takes a few minutes) and then proceed to the instructions in "Rinsing" below.

TIPS FOR SMOOTH PRINTING

- Check the edges of the fabric sheet before printing to make sure the fabric is fully adhered to the backing. If it has come apart (and it sometimes does), simply press it before printing. When you iron the fabric sheet and pick it up, it tends to curl. A curled fabric sheet will easily jam your printer. What we do is iron the sheet and then quickly put it on a cool, flat surface, such as a table, and lay something heavy on top (the old phone-book trick). Once the fabric sheet cools, it will stay flat.
- If the leading edge of the fabric sheet (the end that you put into the printer first) won't stay adhered, try folding a piece of masking tape over the length of that edge.
- If the corners on the leading edge of the fabric sheet catch inside the printer, try clipping the corners before inserting the fabric sheet into the printer.
- Always check the ink levels before printing.

Rinsing

Rinsing the printed image is very important. After printing, there is some excess ink that lies on top of the fabric and in the pile. This ink can be rubbed off or rinsed off at the first washing and can potentially bleed onto adjoining fabric. Each manufacturer of printable fabric sheets has different rinse instructions for their product, but we use a method of rinsing that works for all brands.

The "home-brew" method that we like uses fabric softener and water. It is the same method used by Color Textiles, but we use it successfully on all brands of printable fabric. We believe this method to be best because of the differences in local water all across the country. Some elements in water can have negative effects on ink and printable fabric sheets. Fabric softener helps counteract the effects of various chemicals and other substances that make a difference in water quality. With this method, we have noticed less ink loss and sharper images.

Note: There is one exception to our rinsing method. When you are using Bubble Jet Set 2000 to treat your own fabric, please use the Bubble Jet Rinse.

1. Mix ¼ cup of fabric softener and ¾ cup of water in a plastic tub. We use a big plastic container with a lid so we can save the unused solution. Generally, we mix a batch of about 6 cups of solution at a time (1½ cups of fabric softener, 4½ cups of water). This makes the job easier. We have had the best luck with All and Snuggle brand fabric softeners.

2. After your printed fabric is dry, carefully peel the paper off the back of the printed sheet. Peel evenly on a flat surface to help prevent the fabric from distorting.

3. Submerse the fabric in the solution for about 10 to 15 seconds. Lift it out and let the excess drain back into the tub—you can reuse it several times. You will see some excess ink coming off your fabric; this is normal. Don't wring out the fabric; we did that once and regretted it!

4. Once the fabric drains, lay it on an old towel and lightly blot it to remove the majority of the liquid.

5. Drape the fabric sheets over a drying rack or clothesline and let dry. Press flat after drying. Now you are ready to use your fabric and begin sewing!

PRESSING INSIGHTS

Ironing printable fabric sheets is OK in moderation. We use the steam feature sparingly and usually iron on the wrong side of the print so we don't risk scorching the fabric. Be sure to watch out for irons that "spit"! We have damaged quilts from steam irons that spit hot water on the printed image. Test your iron on something else to avoid ending up with water spots. (However, if you use the rinse formula above, this should not be a problem.) We usually use the silk/wool setting for ironing, but always be careful that you don't scorch your project.

How Tall Are You? 20" x 46"

Care of Quilts

There are a few things you should know regarding the care of printed fabric and the quilts made with it. How you prepare and care for your fabric has a dramatic effect on the longevity of your project. Rinsing, keeping it clean, and protecting it from the elements will really help. This is a special fabric and needs some special attention.

Washing and Drying

When it comes to washing printable fabric, don't expect these fabrics to wash like normal fabrics. No matter what the manufacturers say, printable fabric simply isn't as washable as regular fabric. We often compare printable fabric sheets to hand-dyed fabric. The dyes are not perfectly stable, but they are pretty good. If you wash your project in a washing machine, the printed fabric will fade, no doubt about it. However, with the proper care, projects made with printed fabric will last for generations. If you look at all the projects in this book, it is safe to say that the vast majority of them will not see a washing machine. They may see the fuzzy end of a vacuum brush (used for upholstery), but a washing machine? Not likely. If it is necessary to wash a project, we recommend hand washing in cold water with Orvus Quilt Soap. Dry-cleaning is acceptable, but it does not offer any significant advantage.

Drying your projects in a dryer will lower the quality of your project due to the abrasion against other items or the dryer drum. We typically let our projects line dry and then press them gently. Dry them in a dryer if you must, but we don't do it. The one exception to this rule is silk. Silk is a little stiff when you first print it, rinse it, and sew it, but then it gets wonderfully soft when dried in a machine. We typically dry a silk project in the dryer once, tossing in a towel to add abrasion, and then line dry it from that point on.

Maximizing the Life of Your Project

Sunlight, abrasion, and detergents can be damaging to printed fabrics. Avoid them as much as possible to ensure vivid images for many years to come.

Sunlight. Direct sunlight over a period of time will fade your project. If you hang your project on the wall, choose a location where it doesn't get direct sunlight day after day.

Abrasion. The ink on printable fabric sheets can rub off over a period of time. What are the ramifications of this? If you use a printed panel within an item of children's clothing, for example, the ink will wear off. But if you use the panel in a wall hanging or other type of project for display only, you have nothing to worry about.

Detergents. Simply put, don't use regular detergents, because they are much too harsh. Stick to quilt soap that is available through quilt shops, sewing-machine dealers, and online.

General Quilt Construction

In this section, we discuss the sewing supplies needed to complete the projects, and we cover the steps to piece your poster prints together—you can avoid all the mistakes we have made in the past! For new quilters, we cover basic quilting and binding techniques from start to finish and show you how to create a rod pocket to hang your masterpiece. You may need to refer back to this section throughout your projects for helpful tips and instructions. Have fun with your favorite photographs by printing them onto fabric and creating wonderful quilts and gifts.

Basic Sewing Supplies

The following sewing supplies and tools will make your sewing easier. Each project includes a list of fabrics and additional supplies as needed.

- Appliqué pressing sheet
- Iron
- Rotary cutter, mat, and rulers
- Straight pins and safety pins
- Seam ripper
- Variety of decorative threads for embellishments
- White sewing thread for piecing printed panels
- 80/12 Universal needle (for piecing)

Piecing Printed Poster Images

You can enlarge your photograph to poster size or, as we like to say, "Posterize it!" The first size is a standard 8½" x 11" printable fabric sheet or the maximum size of fabric your printer will allow.

To make larger, poster-sized quilts, you'll need to sew multiple sheets together. (Be sure to remove the paper from the back of the sheets and follow the rinsing instructions on page 27.) The first thing to keep in mind is that the edges of the images aren't always square with the fabric. Be sure to line up the edges of the images and not the fabric. You can trim around the images before sewing, leaving a ¼" seam allowance all around. Also, pin carefully and check before you sew to make sure that the images will match up correctly. If you rip out stitches with a seam ripper, the needle perforations won't "heal" as well as on regular quilting cotton, and the needle holes may show. The fixative, the adhesive on the backing sheet, and the remaining residue on the printable fabric sheet make it less forgiving to rip out. Poplin with a high thread count shows this problem in the worst way. Be sure to use the "frog stitch" in case you have to rip-it, rip-it, rip-it!

Follow the steps below to piece a printed poster together after rinsing and pressing.

1. Re-create the original picture by laying out the printed images on a flat surface.

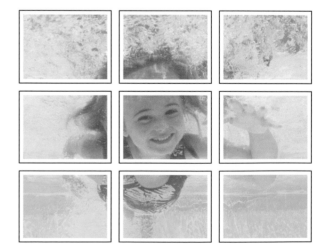

It's helpful to keep the original photograph or your paper test print handy when laying out and sewing the printed fabric sheets so that you can see the overall picture. It's like keeping the box cover nearby when doing a jigsaw puzzle.

2. Thread your sewing machine with white sewing thread and use an 80/12 Universal needle for best results.

3. Start at either the bottom or the top and work from one side to the other. Place two printed panels right sides together. Hold them up to a light so that you can see through them and make sure the printed seam allowances are matched up. Pin the pieces together and then fold open the fabric and check that major elements of the image are lined up properly.

   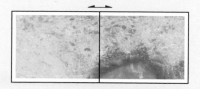

   Another option is to trim and square up your panels before sewing. Use a rotary cutter and ruler to cut ¼" from the printed image all around, making sure the panels or blocks have square corners. You may want to give yourself a slightly larger seam allowance and trim it later. A wider seam allowance may make sewing and matching up the printed seams easier.

4. Sew the two panels together using the edge of the printed image as your guide. Check the alignment once again on the right side. If necessary, make any adjustments now. Then trim the seam allowances to ¼" using a rotary cutter and ruler if you did not already do so.

5. Press the seam allowances open using an iron on the wool/silk setting.

Pressing Advice

Pressing the seam allowance open instead of to one side will make the seams almost invisible from the right side of the quilt. Use an iron set on the wool/silk setting to press the seam allowances open. Then flip the fabric over and, using an appliqué pressing sheet, press the seams from the right side of the quilt so the seam allowances lie flat. Don't iron directly on the printed side—there is too much risk of scorching or having your iron spit water on the image and damage it. Appliqué pressing sheets are available at quilt shops and through mail order. We like these sheets made of Teflon, but if you don't have one, you can also iron carefully using a pressing cloth.

6. Sew together the remaining printed panels to complete the row. Repeat to sew the other rows together.

7. Once all the rows have been sewn, trimmed, and pressed, join the rows. Pin the rows together, matching the printed seam allowance as well as the sewn seams. Remember to fold open the fabric and check that major elements of the image are lined up properly before stitching.

8. Trim any seam allowances to ¼" as needed and press the seam allowances open from the wrong side. Then press the seams from the right side as well, using the appliqué pressing sheet.

9. Square up the edges of your pieced photo, leaving ¼" seam allowances all around.

Adding Borders

We generally stitch borders to the quilt and cut them to fit afterward. In the cutting instructions for each project we have allowed an extra 1" to 2" in case your quilt measures a bit different from ours. You may want to wait until the center of your quilt is complete and then measure it before cutting and adding borders. You may also decide that you want your border to be a different width than the quilt shown.

Quilting

The focus of your quilt should be the photograph, and the way you quilt around the images should emphasize and complement the photos. The quilting styles and battings we recommend may not be what you use for traditional quilting projects, but we have done lots of experimentation and these are the battings and quilting options that we have found to be most successful for poster quilts.

Choosing Batting

To highlight the photographs, we generally use limited quilting so that the stitches don't detract from the printed image. If you do minimal quilting on a wall hanging, you have to select a batting that will support the work. We've found that fusible fleece and fusible batting work best to prevent the image from bagging or sagging when hung for a period of time. They also allow you to avoid pin basting. Don't pin baste through the image; the holes may show after pins are removed. Fusible fleece has a little stiffer feel

to it. However, it works great to give a photo image the body and stability needed to hang on a wall. If you are making a poster quilt that is larger than 2 panels x 2 panels, stability is essential for good results.

Use fusible batting for items that you want to have a softer feel to them. You can also use regular batting for items that will not be hung on a wall. Also choose a high-loft batting for more dimension or the look of trapunto. Most of the projects shown in this book were made using fusible fleece to give a crisp look and prevent the image from distorting when hung.

Stitch-in-the-Ditch Quilting

We use this traditional quilting method in most of our projects in any border seams or sashing seams. You can use a thread color that matches your quilt fabric or use monofilament, as we usually do, because it works with fabric of any color.

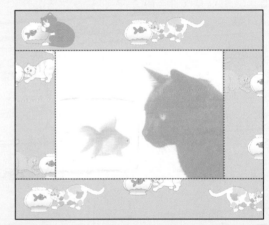

> **TIP**
>
> If you have a stitch-in-the-ditch foot for your sewing machine, this will make your sewing easier. This foot has a flange in the center that follows the groove of the seam allowance.

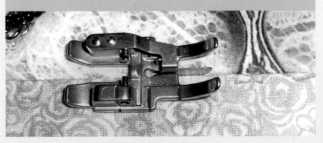

Outline Quilting with Monofilament

We used monofilament, or transparent thread, to quilt most of the projects in this book. The majority of photo quilts are generally people or animals, so using a colored thread, especially over a person's face, would not be ideal. Threading the monofilament in the needle and winding regular sewing thread on the bobbin to match the quilt backing allows you to quilt the photograph without the thread showing.

Note: We don't recommend using monofilament for quilting baby quilts. Choose a cotton or cotton-wrapped polyester thread, which will be softer.

By sewing around an image with monofilament, you can create a trapunto look. It raises the image slightly, which makes it look like you have trapunto quilted your image. Use a higher-loft batting, if you prefer, to make the image even more prominent. (Free-motion quilting around the image is easier than straight stitching because you avoid having to constantly turn the quilt.)

Detail of "Remembering Grandma Bredeson" showing stitching around the button image

Bartacking

If you don't want any specific part of your image to pop out, a bar tack will hold the layers together while being virtually invisible. Use monofilament and set your sewing machine to stitch a small, narrow zigzag. Drop the feed dogs to prevent the quilt layers from moving. Set the stitch width to 0 first and take three stitches to lock the thread. Increase the stitch width to 2.5 or 3 and take about eight stitches. Decrease the width to 0 and take another three stitches to lock the thread. If your machine has a button-sew feature, it will do this for you automatically. Randomly stitch a bar tack about every 6" across the quilt to hold the layers together. We used this technique in almost all the quilts, especially around and through images of people's faces.

Free-Motion Quilting

Free-motion quilting can be a lot of fun. Drop the feed dogs on your sewing machine, and use a darning foot. You control the direction and length of stitching so that you can quilt curves, swirls, and other designs quickly and easily without having to rotate the quilt under the machine. If you have never tried this technique before, practice first until you can maintain a constant speed for an even stitch length. You may have to adjust the tension, depending on the thread and fabric you are using. When starting and stopping, take three or four stitches in the same space to lock the threads.

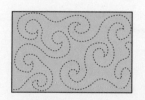 

START SLOWLY

If you are a beginner, use the half-speed or "sew slow" adjustment if your machine has it. This will give you a good tempo to start with. It takes practice to maintain a fluid movement. If you move the fabric too fast, you will have long jump stitches. If you move the fabric too slowly, you will have tiny little stitches. With this technique, practice makes perfect.

Quilting with Embroidery

You can also use embroidery as a quilting technique. On "Sunflower Girl" (page 21), we used an outline-embroidery design to quilt the layers together. It creates a pattern and is easier than free-motion quilting. You can embroider before or after you have attached your binding.

Select an embroidery design that is somewhat open and works with the theme of your photograph. Follow your instruction manual to load the embroidery design onto your machine. It's not necessary to use a stabilizer, when embroidering the three layers of a quilt sandwich, but generally, the stiffer the fabric, the better the stitch quality. Use a wash-away stabilizer, if desired, for easy removal after stitching. If you are embroidering the quilt top only, you can use a tear-away stabilizer since you will not see it inside the quilt.

OVERLAPPING DESIGNS

Try embroidering a design so that it is partially on top of the printed image and partially on the border. You can also quilt around the embroidery design or embroider over quilting stitches.

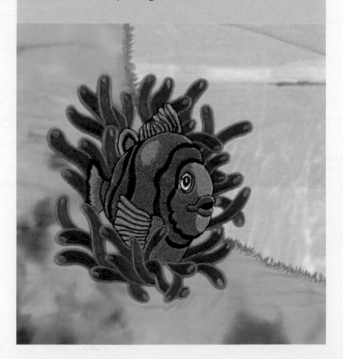

Quilting with Decorative Stitching

We often use decorative stitching to appliqué an image to the background fabric, but you can also use decorative stitching for quilting to create texture and add dimension. Most sewing machines have lots of wonderful decorative stitches that are great for embellishment. Select a fun decorative stitch and follow these tips for best results.

- Set the needle tension at 3 and do a test on practice fabric first.
- If you are sewing around a shape, choose a decorative stitch that does not have a lot of intricate details to the pattern. Sometimes the weight of the quilt can make it drag and distort the stitch pattern.
- If your machine has a single-stitch pattern with the needle down, this will make sewing a perfect pattern easier. When you use this option, your machine will complete one of the designs and stop with the needle down; this is the time to pivot your fabric at the corners and around a shape.
- If you pivot your fabric as you are sewing, the stitch can become distorted.
- Try using some of the wonderful decorative threads that are available: 30-weight cottons, variegated cotton and rayon threads, as well as embroidery threads. You can save time by using a prewound bobbin for embroidery.

The stained-glass quilt was stitched with gold metallic thread in the needle.

- Always use stabilizer behind the fabrics to prevent puckering. Use a wash-away stabilizer such as Aqua Magic by Inspira or Ultra Solvy by Sulky and tear it away after stitching.
- Mist any remaining bits of wash-away stabilizer with water to remove them.
- Starch your quilt top and backing before layering and basting. This helps stabilize your fabric and ensure a good stitch quality.

FOR FUN ONLY

Decorative stitching for embellishment purposes is easier if done on the quilt top only. Use a tear-away stabilizer when stitching the top only.

Quilting with Embellishments

Another method you can use to quilt a wall hanging is to tack on or sew on three-dimensional objects through all three layers. Look at "Remembering Grandma Bredeson" on page 44. It not only has a trapuntoed look from the quilting, but it also includes vintage buttons sewn through all three layers. The buttons add interest and dimension and serve as quilting as well, holding the layers together where they are attached. You can sew almost any type of object onto your quilt—silk flowers, beads, family heirlooms that relate to your photograph, or objects such as earrings that work with the theme of your quilt project.

EMBELLISHMENTS

Embellishments such as lace edgings or other pieces of fabric can be added to create texture when your quilt top is complete. On the quilt "Remembering Grandma Bredeson," we attached lace trims across the quilt top to go with the theme of the quilt. You can stitch the lace on with matching thread using a straight stitch or free-motion stitching. Have fun applying all types of trims, beads, buttons, sequins, and so on to your quilt to create the look that's perfect for you. If you have a quilt with a Mardi Gras theme, you might attach sequin trim crystals to create a festive look. Add three-dimensional embellishments after the machine quilting is done.

Crystals glint from the panes of a stained-glass quilt.

Crocheted lace added as embellishment enhances the vintage feel of this tribute quilt.

Creating a Rod Pocket

If you plan to make a quilted wall hanging, you will need to create a rod pocket or hanging sleeve for the back of your quilt. Attach the rod pocket after quilting, before you add the binding.

1. Cut an 8"-wide strip of fabric to a length 1" less than the width of your quilt. Use leftover backing fabric or another coordinating fabric.

2. Fold under ¼" along the short ends of the fabric and fold under ¼" again to create a finished edge. Topstitch the hem on both sides.

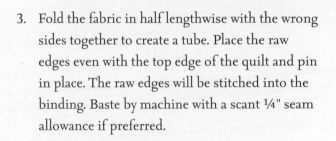

3. Fold the fabric in half lengthwise with the wrong sides together to create a tube. Place the raw edges even with the top edge of the quilt and pin in place. The raw edges will be stitched into the binding. Baste by machine with a scant ¼" seam allowance if preferred.

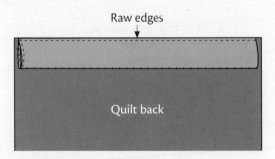

Raw edges

Quilt back

Binding Techniques

Binding is a way to cover or encase the raw edges of the quilt top, batting, and backing with strips of fabric. We prefer double-fold binding, cut on the crosswise grain. This is the easiest method; it saves on fabric, and the strips will have just a little stretch to them (lengthwise grain does not stretch at all). For quilts with curved edges, use bias binding so it will have more stretch to ease around the curves; see page 38.

Binding gives your quilt a finished look, like a picture frame for your photographs. You may want the frame to jump out from your finished project, but in most of our quilt examples, we wanted the photograph to be the main feature and so we chose binding fabric that would blend in with the borders and not be a main focal point of the quilt. You can choose fabric of any color or print you like for your binding. Remember to attach a rod pocket before binding if you plan to hang your quilt.

Straight-Grain Binding

1. Using a rotary cutter, ruler, and cutting mat, cut 2¼"-wide strips across the width of the fabric. Each project will tell you how many strips to cut, but you will need enough to go around your quilt with about 12" extra for joining strips and mitering the corners.

2. Sew the binding strips together with a diagonal seam, placing them right sides together and perpendicular to each other as shown. Stitch from corner to corner and trim the seam allowance to ¼". Press the seam allowance open.

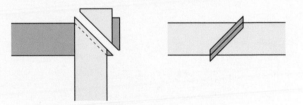

3. Fold the binding strip in half lengthwise, wrong sides together, and press.

4. Set up your sewing machine for straight stitching with monofilament in the needle and all-purpose thread that matches your quilt backing fabric in the bobbin. Using a ¼" quilting foot along with the dual-feed option (built-in walking foot) achieves good results. If your machine does not have a built-in walking foot, we suggest attaching a walking foot so the layers will feed through evenly.

5. With your quilt right side up, begin in the middle of one side of your quilt and align the raw edge of the binding with the raw edge of the quilt sandwich. Leaving a 6" tail of binding unstitched, sew the binding to the quilt using a ¼" seam allowance. Sew down the first side of the quilt, stopping ¼" from the first corner. Pivot your quilt top 90° and sew off the edge.

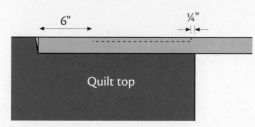

6. Fold the binding strip up so the fold forms a 45° angle, as shown. Then fold the strip back down so it is lined up with the next side of the quilt. Begin sewing at the folded edge and stitch the second side of the quilt. Stop ¼" from the next corner.

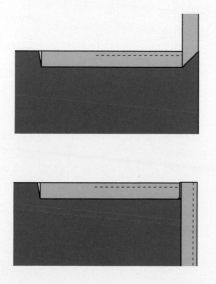

7. Repeat steps 5 and 6 until you are about 8" from where you started stitching. Pin the binding tails to the quilt until they meet in the middle, and press to make a crease where they meet. Trim one of the binding tails along the crease; cut the remaining binding tail 2¼" beyond the crease. (This distance is equal to the width you cut your binding.)

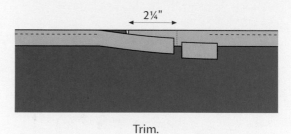

Trim.

8. Open up the binding tails and sew them together, placing them right sides together and perpendicular to each other as you did in step 2. Stitch from corner to corner, trim the seam allowance to ¼", and press open. Refold the binding and finish sewing it to the quilt.

9. Press the binding to the back of the quilt, creating a diagonal fold, or miter, at each corner. Press the binding flat and place pins in the corners and where necessary to hold the mitered shape. Make sure the folded edge of the binding covers the stitching on the back of the quilt.

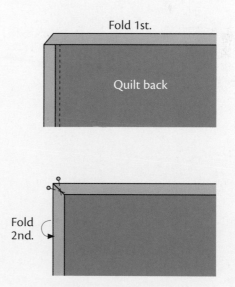

10. From the right side of the quilt, straight stitch into the quilt top, right next to the binding. You should also be stitching the folded edge of the binding on the back. Sew a few inches and check to make sure you are catching the binding on the back. A stitch-in-the-ditch foot makes this easier. Take your time when pivoting at the corners to catch the miters. After you have sewn around the quilt, remove it from the machine and check to make sure you have sewn the binding down completely. You have now finished the binding and are ready for any last-minute three-dimensional embellishments!

Bias Binding

Bias binding is great for quilts with shaped or curved edges. Strips cut on the bias (at a 45° angle) have more stretch to them and will go around curves nicely.

1. Cut 2¼"-wide strips using a ruler with a 45° angle on it.

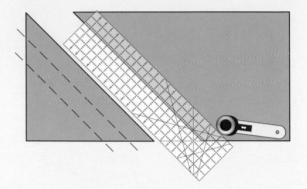

2. Piece bias strips on the diagonal as shown with a ¼" seam allowance. Press the seam allowance open and follow steps 3–10 of "Straight-Grain Binding" on page 36.

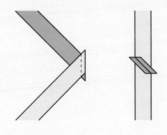

Detail of **Feathered Nostalgia** by Ellen Pahl, 30" x 31"

Projects

In this section are five fun and different poster quilts to choose from. The first one is quick and easy, ideal for testing the waters of photo printing. Each project highlights a different style of quilt construction yielding a different effect. Now that you have learned all you need to know to produce a great posterized image—let's get started sewing!

Note: Measurements and dimensions of your quilt may be slightly different from ours. There are many variables that will have an effect on dimensions. Variables range from the size and proportion of your original photo image to the way it prints out on fabric. Since printers and software applications vary in the way they print photos onto fabric sheets, you could have more or less white space to trim from your printed fabric sheets. If your images vary considerably, you may need to recalculate yardage amounts. The yardage and supplies we've listed are generous, but always do a test print on paper to see how your posterized print compares to the one in the project shown. You may want to wait to cut any border pieces until the center of the quilt is complete.

TIPS TO REMEMBER

Here are a few things to keep in mind before starting your poster project.

- Always print your poster on paper first before using your fabric. Lay all the pieces on the floor or table to check that everything is the way you want it.
- When choosing a photo for a poster print, think ahead to how many sections you will want to split the photo into. This will help you choose the best photo and avoid seam lines falling right in the middle of a subject's face.
- Remember that images don't always print squarely on the fabric. When lining up pieces of the poster, use the edges of the image, not the edges of the fabric, as your sewing guide.
- Use manufacturer's original ink for your finished prints. Save refills or remanufactured cartridges for everyday use.
- These would not be great projects for baby quilts because baby quilts need to withstand frequent washings. There is also a chance that the printed image could run if the baby puts the quilt in his or her mouth.

The Patient Kitty

By Frankie Seme ~ Finished Size: 16" x 13½" ~ Number of Panels: 1

This is the easiest of all poster quilts—you simply enlarge a photo to the full size of the fabric sheet. This quilt requires no piecing of the image, so you can choose any favorite photo and have fun learning the techniques.

Materials

Yardages are based on *42"-wide fabric.*
1 printable fabric sheet, 8½" x 11"
¾ yard of multicolored print for border and backing
¼ yard of fabric for binding
16" x 18" piece of fusible fleece
2 plastic rings, ½" diameter, for hanging quilt
Optional machine-embroidery supplies:
    Embroidery designs
    Decorative thread
    12" x 12" piece of Tear-A-Way-Lite stabilizer

Cutting

From the multicolored print, cut:

2 strips, 3" x 10"
2 strips, 3" x 18"
1 piece, 16" x 18"

From the binding fabric, cut:

2 strips, 2¼" x 40"

Image Creation

There are many ways to enlarge a photo to an 8½" x 11"
fabric sheet. We'll walk you through the process using a
computer with the Microsoft Windows operating system or
an all-in-one printer, but you can print from any program
you're comfortable using.

Computer with Windows

This is one of the easiest methods we have found, using
a common feature found on most PCs (Windows-based
computers)—the picture and fax viewer. Your photo needs
to be scanned into your computer or downloaded from a
digital camera.

1. To use this feature, locate your picture on your computer
   and right-click with your mouse. Choose Open With and
   Windows Picture and Fax Viewer as shown in figure 1.

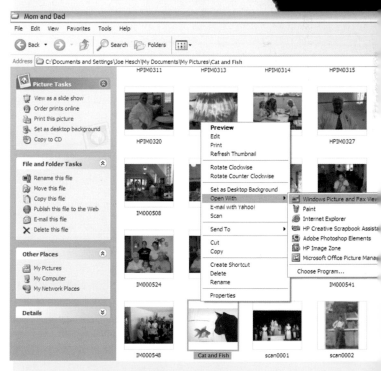

Fig. 1—*Microsoft product screen shot reprinted with permission from Microsoft Corporation.*

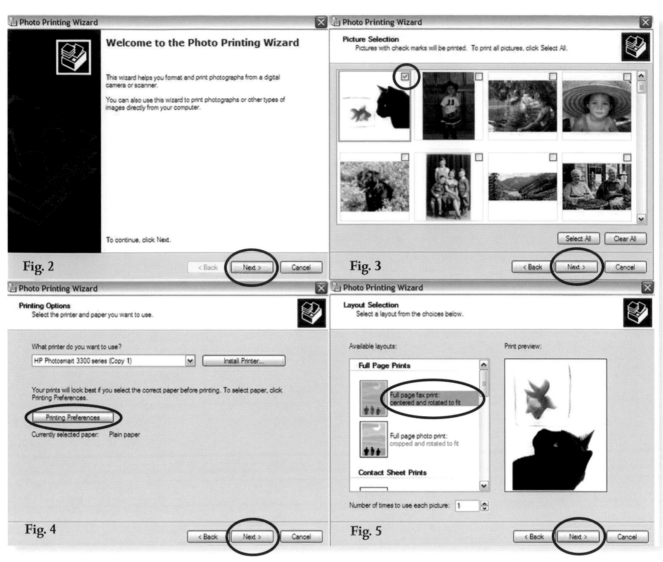

Microsoft product screen shots reprinted with permission from Microsoft Corporation.

2. Click on the Print icon at the bottom and follow the instructions of the Photo Printing Wizard (figs. 2–4). Select "Full page fax print" and print the first full page onto paper (fig. 5).

3. Practice with this tool to print your image on paper; you will soon find it very easy. When you are ready to print on fabric, set the print quality to Best and your paper type to Plain by clicking on the Printing Preferences tab. Insert a fabric sheet into the printer and print.

4. Carefully remove the paper backing from the printed iimage. (Peel the paper off evenly so the image does not become distorted.)

5. Refer to "Rinsing" on page 27 to remove excess ink from the fabric sheet.

6. Using a rotary cutter and ruler, trim the printed panel, leaving a ¼" seam allowance all around.

All-in-One Copier

Another option is to use the Reduce/Enlarge feature on an all-in-one copier.

1. Simply lay your photograph on the scanner bed, select Reduce/Enlarge, and select Entire Page.

2. Copy onto paper to check the quality of the image.

3. When you're satisfied with the image, insert a fabric sheet and repeat the procedure—it's easy!

4. Follow steps 4–6 of the section "Computer with Windows" on page 41.

Sewing Instructions

1. Sew the 3" x 10" border strips to the right and left sides of the fabric panel using a ¼" seam allowance. Using a rotary cutter and ruler, trim the excess border strips even with the edges of the photograph. With your iron set on the wool/silk setting, press the seam allowances toward the border fabric.

2. Sew the remaining border strips to the top and bottom of the quilt. Trim the border strips and press the seam allowances toward the border.

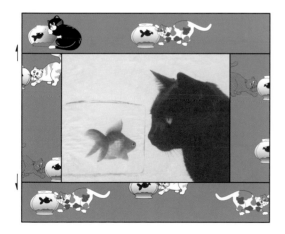

3. Using an appliqué pressing sheet or pressing cloth to protect your iron, fuse the fleece to the wrong side of your quilt top. The rough side of the fleece is the fusible side.

4. Optional embroidery: Set up your machine for embroidery and load an embroidery design that coordinates with the theme of your picture. (Follow the instructions that came with your embroidery machine.) Insert your quilt and stabilizer into a hoop. You can embroider through the printed image to create dimension and character.

5. When embroidery is complete, remove the excess stabilizer from the back of the quilt and trim the thread that links one part of the design to another.

Finishing the Quilt

1. Place the backing wrong side up on a flat surface and layer the quilt and fleece on top, photo side facing up. Use safety pins in the borders to hold the three layers in place for quilting.

2. Quilt the layers, stitching in the ditch of the border seams. Quilt the borders as desired. Refer to "Quilting" on page 32 for additional details.

3. Using a ruler and rotary cutter, square up the edges of your quilt.

4. Bind the quilt using your favorite method, or see "Binding Techniques" on page 36.

5. Place the two small plastic rings about ½" from the top of the quilt. Sew them by hand, or by machine with the button-sew feature or a small zigzag stitch (3.5mm). Drop the feed dogs so the fabric does not move as you sew.

Three-Dimensional Collage

Remembering
Grandma Bredeson

By Frankie Seme ~ Finished Size: 28" x 23" ~ Number of Panels: 4, set 2 x 2

This quilt is based on an arrangement of items that belonged to Joe's great grandmother—a tatting shuttle, some tatting, eyeglasses, buttons, a thimble, a Bible, and a photo of her with Joe's great grandfather. It is made of four panels sewn together without sashing. This technique lends itself to many themes—a wedding, a baby shower, a sports-card collection, or a fishing motif, to name just a few.

Materials

Yardages are based on 42"-wide fabric.

4 printable fabric sheets, 8½" x 11"

⅔ yard of fabric for border and binding

⅞ yard of fabric for backing

27" x 32" piece of fusible fleece or fusible batting

Optional embellishments:

    Buttons, ribbons, vintage lace, jewelry

Cutting

From the border and binding fabric, cut:

2 strips, 4" x 18"

2 strips, 4" x 30"

3 strips, 2¼" x 40"

From the backing fabric, cut:

1 piece, 26" x 32"

Image Creation

We used a technique called "3-D scanning" or "3-D copying" to create the image for this quilt. You're probably familiar with scanning photos and artwork, but did you know you could put other things on your scanner/copier? People don't typically think of scanners being used in this manner, but it is really easy and you can create some nice collages. In the quilt shown, Joe had the help of his mom, Dorie, and used some memorabilia from his great-grandmother Louise. Arrange the items as you like and do a test print. You may find you need to rearrange items slightly to get just the right effect. It doesn't take long and is a fun, creative process. Take a look at the photo at right, showing the flowers we scanned. See also page 10 for a quilt made from similar scans.

We have scanned all sorts of things, from jewelry, toys, and seashells to food and candy. Once you get the image looking just the way you want it, print it

You can arrange flowers and other three-dimensional items on your scanner bed to create collage images.

into a poster on four fabric sheets using the method of your choice. As always, make a test print on paper first.

Note: It is best if you scan the image and print it using your computer. You can print directly onto fabric from the scanner bed, but it may print closer to the edges of the fabric, requiring a narrow seam allowance when you sew the panels together.

SCANNER PROTECTION

If you are scanning anything that is abrasive, protect the glass of your scanner bed by placing a protective sheet of plastic down first. We use overhead transparency sheets available from office-supply stores.

Sewing Instructions

1. Arrange the four panels and sew them together, following the instructions in "Piecing Printed Poster Images" on page 30.

2. Sew a 4" x 18" border strip to each side of the quilt using a ¼" seam allowance. Trim the extra length so the borders are even with the quilt top. Using an iron on the wool/silk setting, press the seam allowance toward the border so that it lies nice and flat.

3. Sew the 4" x 30" border strips to the top and bottom. Trim and press as before.

4. Add any flat embellishments at this point. We added some beautiful lace trim to dress up the quilt top. You can simply topstitch the lace in place.

Finishing the Quilt

1. Fuse the fleece or batting to the wrong side of the quilt top. (The bumpy side of the fleece is the fusible side.)

2. Place the quilt top on the wrong side of the backing and baste with safety pins in the borders for machine quilting.

3. Quilt the layers, stitching in the ditch of the border seams. Use free-motion quilting or quilt as desired in the borders.

4. To secure the four-panel printed image, we randomly bartacked across the image to hold the layers together; refer to "Bartacking" on page 33. You can also free-motion quilt around the images with monofilament to give it the trapunto look.

5. Press the quilt top gently with a pressing cloth. Square up the edges and corners of your quilt using a ruler and rotary cutter. Add a rod pocket and binding, referring to "Creating a Rod Pocket" and "Binding Techniques" on page 36.

6. See "Quilting with Embellishments" on page 35 for techniques to add buttons or other items to the quilt.

North Dakota Hunting

By Frankie Seme ~ Finished Size: 41" x 34" ~ Number of Panels: 9, set 3 x 3

Here's a chance to make a scrapbook-style quilt using a software collage program, such as the HP Creative Scrapbook Assistant. The quilt is made of nine panels, which can be sewn together with or without sashing. You can be as creative as you like, adding embroidered items, three-dimensional embellishments, and quilting with decorative threads. Another option is to quilt around the photos or shapes to give them a trapunto look.

Materials

Yardages are based on *42"-wide fabric.*
9 printable fabric sheets, 8½" x 11"
¾ yard of fabric for outer border
½ yard of fabric for inner border and binding
1⅜ yards of fabric for backing
38" x 45" piece of fusible fleece or fusible batting

Cutting

From the inner-border and binding fabric, cut:
4 strips, 1½" x 40"
4 strips, 2¼" x 40"

From the outer-border fabric, cut:
5 strips, 4½" x 40"

From the backing fabric, cut:
1 piece, 38" x 45"

Image Creation

We used HP Creative Scrapbook Assistant software for this project. It's one of our favorites because it's great for making collages and has nice features, such as the option to create a picture within a picture, a variety of frames to place around pictures, and the ability to add text to the project. We won't take you step by step through the program's features; almost any scrapbooking software or desktop-publishing software you currently use will work just fine. Go with what you are comfortable with and what works well for you. Just remember that once you have designed your project, it is important to do a test print on paper using the poster print function to see how it looks. Once you are satisfied with the results, print the image on fabric sheets, and refer to "Rinsing" on page 27.

Sewing Instructions

1. Piece your printed images together as described in "Piecing Printed Poster Images" on page 30. Trim and square up the quilt top, leaving a ¼" seam allowance.

2. Sew a 1½"-wide inner-border strip to opposite sides of the quilt top using a ¼" seam allowance. Trim away the excess length so the borders are even with the quilt top. Press the seam allowances toward the borders. Sew the remaining inner-border strips to the top and bottom of the quilt. Trim and press.

3. Sew a 4½"-wide outer-border strip to opposite sides of the quilt top in the same manner as for the inner borders. Trim the excess fabric and press. Sew the remaining three outer-border strips together, pressing the seam allowances to one side. Cut the strip in half and sew the strips to the top and bottom of the quilt. Trim and press.

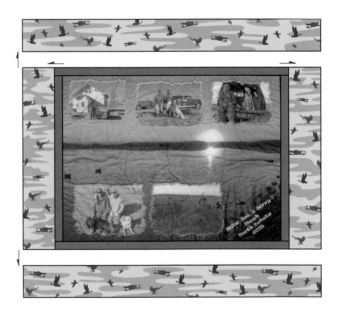

Finishing the Quilt

1. Square up your quilt top and fuse the fleece or batting to the wrong side of it.

2. Place the backing fabric on a flat surface, wrong side up, and place the fleece or batting on top to create the quilt sandwich.

3. Safety pin the layers together in the borders to prepare for quilting.

4. Quilt the layers, stitching in the ditch of the borders; quilt as desired in the borders.

5. Press the quilt top gently, using a pressing cloth. With a ruler and rotary cutter, square up the edges and corners.

6. Add a rod pocket if desired, referring to page 36. Bind the quilt using your favorite method, or see "Binding Techniques" on page 36.

Stained-Glass Art

By Frankie Seme ~ Finished Size: 40" x 54" ~ Number of Panels: 16, set 4 x 4

We love stained-glass windows and thought that this photo would lend itself well to a creative and dramatic quilt using the posterizing technique and windowpane sashing. Frankie purchased the photograph online (see "Resources" on page 63).

Materials

Yardages are based on *42"-wide fabric.*

16 printable fabric sheets, 8½" x 11"

2⅓ yards of dark cotton fabric for background, sashing, and binding

2⅞ yards of cotton fabric for backing*

44" x 58" piece of fusible fleece or fusible batting

Appliqué pressing sheet

5¾ yards of ¼"-wide Steam-A-Seam strips (double-sided fusible tape)

2½ yards of fusible web (17" wide)

Machine-embroidery thread

Tear-away stabilizer

Chalk marker or chalk wheel

Gold metallic thread

Small plastic rings

Optional:

    Crystals

    Fabric glue

If your fabric is wide enough for an unpieced backing, 1⅞ yards will be enough.

Cutting

From the dark cotton fabric, cut:

1 rectangle, 42" x 56"

5 strips, 1½" x 42"

5 strips, 2¼" x 42"

Image Creation

Print the photo using the poster function in the print driver, or you can create it using one of the methods described in "Four Ways to Posterize a Photo" on page 23.

Sewing Instructions

1. Piece the panels of your printed image together as described in "Piecing Printed Poster Images" on page 30.

2. Apply the fusible web to the back of the pieced panels, following the manufacturer's instructions and making sure to cover the entire surface. Allow to cool.

Photography Web sites have many beautiful photos with high resolution. You can, of course, take your own photo of a stained-glass window or any other subject that could appear to be seen through a window.

3. Trim the pieced image from the right side into the desired shape. To create the look of a stained-glass window, we cut the top of the quilt in a window shape, but depending on your photo you could use a rectangle, square, circle, or an irregular shape if desired.

4. Place the 42" x 56" background fabric on a flat surface, right side up. Center your newly shaped image on the background fabric and fuse into place. Be sure to use the appliqué pressing sheet on top of the image and follow the manufacturer's instructions for fusing.

5. To make the sashing tubes for the windowpanes, use a ¼" foot if you have one, and sew a 1½"-wide dark strip with wrong sides together down the long sides. Press the seam allowance open and the tube flat, turning it so that the seam allowance

is on the back side of the tube and will not show. Repeat this process with the remaining 1½"-wide strips.

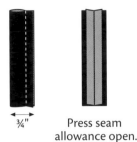

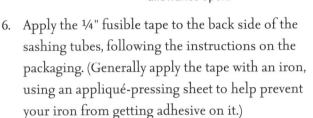

¾"   Press seam allowance open.

6. Apply the ¼" fusible tape to the back side of the sashing tubes, following the instructions on the packaging. (Generally apply the tape with an iron, using an appliqué-pressing sheet to help prevent your iron from getting adhesive on it.)

7. Peel the paper off the back of the fusible web. The tubes can now be fused into place for sewing. On an ironing board, position three of the tubes horizontally to cover the seams. Trim the tubes to the length needed and press them into place using an appliqué pressing sheet.

FOR PRECISE PLACEMENT

Once you press the fusible web it is permanent, so take the time to line the tubes up correctly the first time.

8. After the horizontal sashing tubes are fused, apply the other two sashing tubes vertically in the same manner. We did not place these tubes over the seams but centered them on the quilt evenly. You can either cover the seams or place the sashing where you would like it to be.

9. Topstitch the sashing into place by machine, sewing down each side.

Decorative Stitching

1. Pin the tear-away stabilizer underneath the quilt top where you will be stitching, and then using machine-embroidery thread, stitch around the appliquéd image to cover the raw edges. Use a decorative machine stitch and sew half on the image and half on the background fabric. (See the photo on page 53.)

2. After stitching around the appliqué once, change to a different color embroidery thread or a gold metallic thread on the top and select another decorative stitch. Outline the stained-glass image a second time to create added details and interest. For more information, see "Quilting with Decorative Stitching" on page 34.

Optional: You can also add machine embroidery to the quilt now or when quilting to give it more dimension. See "Quilting with Embroidery" on page 34 for more information.

Finishing the Quilt

1. Cut and piece the backing fabric so that you have a piece that is at least 44" x 58".

2. Layer the backing, batting, and quilt top, and baste the layers together with safety pins. Do not pin through your printed image—doing so will leave holes that won't repair very well. Use fusible fleece or fusible batting to avoid using pins.

3. Using a chalk marker or chalk wheel, draw quilting lines on the background. You be the artist and decide where you want the quilting to appear. For the stained-glass quilt, we drew lines radiating from the window. Set up your sewing machine for free-motion quilting or straight stitch. Use gold metallic thread in the needle and use thread to match your backing fabric in the bobbin. Carefully quilt across your quilt following the marked lines.

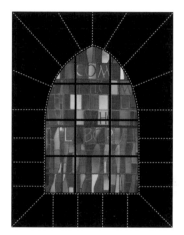

4. You can apply pre-glued crystals to your quilt top to add more dimension or detail using a tool that resembles a woodburning tool. Or apply crystals using fabric glue.

5. With a ruler and rotary cutter, square up the bottom corners of your quilt. Trim the top of the quilt to echo the shape of your image. We trimmed our quilt approximately 8" beyond the stained-glass image all around.

6. Bind the quilt using your favorite method, or see "Binding Techniques" on page 36. A traditional rod pocket won't work for this quilt, so bartack small plastic rings on the back for hanging as described on page 43.

California Coast

By Frankie Seme ~ Finished Size: 44" x 43" ~ Number of Panels: 20, set 4 x 5

When making an Attic Windows project, your choice of photo is critical to the success of the quilt. Photos with intricate detail don't work very well because the sashing "covers up" quite a bit of the photo. In our experience, landscapes seem to work best. Another important point to consider is the number of panels. Due to the sashing, we have found that posters made of 16 fabric sheets (4 x 4) or more are the best choices.

Materials

Yardages are based on *42"-wide fabric.*
20 printable fabric sheets, 8½" x 11"
1⅔ yards of light fabric for block borders and
    outer border*
1⅔ yards of medium fabric for outer border*
1 yard of dark fabric for block borders and binding
1½ yards of fabric for backing
47" x 48" piece of fusible fleece or fusible batting

*Yardage allows for borders to be cut lengthwise. If you
prefer to piece your borders, you will need 1 yard of light
fabric and ½ yard of medium fabric.*

Cutting

Depending on the size of your printed image, the
cutting of the attic-window block borders may vary.
We trimmed our blocks to 7½" x 5½", so we cut
2½" x 10" and 2½" x 12" strips. To determine the
length to cut, add the block border width (2½") plus
at least 2" extra to the block dimensions so your strips
will be long enough to create the mitered corner.

From the light fabric, cut:
2 strips, 4½" x 54", from the lengthwise grain*
20 strips, 2½" x 10"

From the dark fabric, cut:
20 strips, 2½" x 12"
5 strips, 2¼" x 40"

From the medium fabric, cut:
2 strips, 4½" x 54", from the lengthwise grain*

*For pieced borders, cut 3 strips crosswise and piece them
together. Then cut into 2 strips, 54" long.*

Image Creation

To create this image, we simply printed the photo
using the poster function in the print driver. You can

create it using one of the methods described in "Four
Ways to Posterize a Photo" on page 23.

The blocks in an Attic Windows quilt must all be
the same size. As always, do a test print on paper. The
difference between the sizes of the printed images
should be no more than ½". If it is, your image will be
distorted and you should select another photo. You may
need to adjust the cropping of the photo and do a few
test prints before you are ready to print on fabric. Always
mock up your project before you print it on fabric.

This is what our photo looked like when posterized and printed
on paper. The printed areas are all very similar in size.

This photo would not work well for an Attic Windows quilt. When printed
using the poster function, it has much more white space along the top and
bottom rows than in the middle row. It would distort the picture too much
to cut away the photo to make all your blocks uniform.

Preparing the Printed Panels

Once you have printed onto fabric, follow the instructions in "Rinsing" on page 27.

1. Trim around the printed images, leaving ¼" seam allowances.

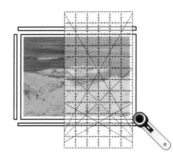

2. If some of your printed panels are smaller or larger than others, measure them all to find the smallest panel and write down these dimensions. Use this measurement and trim a second time to make all the blocks (panels) equal in size. Trim from the bottom and left side of the blocks only.

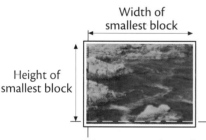

Trim no more than ½".

Smallest block

3. Lay out the panels to form the completed photo. Make sure they are in the correct order. Beginning at the upper-left corner, flip each block over, one at a time, and number it in the top left-hand corner just inside the printed image. This will enable you to find the top of each panel and keep the panels in the correct order throughout the piecing process.

4. You will need to cut a third time to complete the process. Since we are using a 2" finished border on the left side and the bottom of each block to create the Attic Window pattern, we need to trim the left side and the bottom of each block so the picture does not look distorted. One by one, use your rotary cutter and ruler to cut 2" off the left side and 2" off the bottom of each block. Take your time and make sure the photo is right side up.

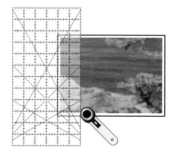

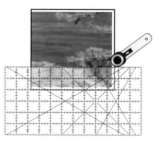

Creating the Attic Windows Blocks

1. Place a 2½" x 10" light strip on the left side of the block, right sides together. Leave approximately 2" in extra length on the bottom of the strip for mitering. Using a ¼" seam allowance and beginning at the top of the strip, sew. Stop ¼" from the bottom and backstitch. Press the seam allowance toward the border.

2. Align a 2½" x 12" dark strip along the bottom of the block, right sides together, and sew across the bottom using a ¼" seam allowance and starting exactly where you left off on the other strip. Lock in your stitching where you start by setting your stitch length at 0, and then slowly increase it to normal. Press the seam allowance toward the border. The strips will overlap and extend beyond each other.

3. Fold the block on the diagonal and lay the strips flat. Turn the seams of the strips so that they temporarily point toward the block; draw a 45° angle on the light strip with a ruler and pencil. Stitch along the drawn line, beginning at the crease where your stitching should meet the previous stitching; sew all the way to the outer edge of the strips. Trim the seam allowance to ¼" and press the seam allowance open.

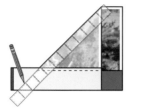 

4. Repeat this process with all 20 blocks. Square up the blocks if needed.

Assembling the Quilt Top

1. Lay out your blocks to form the photo (referring to the numbers on the back corners to help). Beginning with the top row, sew the blocks together into rows using a ¼" seam allowance. Press the seam allowances toward the borders.

    Note: Check the rows as you sew to make sure that no white from the seam allowance is showing.

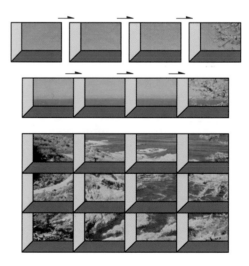

2. Sew the rows together, making sure to match seams and mitered corners. Press the seam allowances toward the border fabrics.

3. Pin a light outer-border strip to the top of the quilt, leaving an extra 6" or more of fabric hanging off both ends. Sew with a ¼" seam allowance, starting and stopping ¼" from both ends and locking in your stitching where you start and stop. Repeat this process to add the second light outer-border strip to the right edge of the quilt.

4. Repeat step 3 to add the medium border strips to the bottom and left edges.

5. Miter all four corners of the quilt as you did for the Attic Windows blocks. Mark the 45° angle, stitch, trim, and press. Press the mitered seam allowances open and the border seam allowances toward the outer borders.

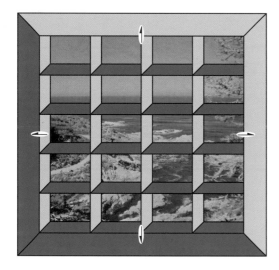

Finishing the Quilt

1. Iron the fusible fleece or batting to the wrong side of the quilt top and then layer the quilt backing fabric with wrong sides together to create your quilt sandwich.

2. Safety pin the layers together for quilting, but do not pin through the printed images. Insert pins in the borders only.

3. Quilt in the ditch of all the border seams and quilt the borders as desired.

4. Press the quilt with a pressing cloth and use a ruler and rotary cutter to square up the edges.

5. Add a rod pocket, if desired, referring to page 36. Use the dark strips to bind the quilt using your favorite method, or see "Binding Techniques" on page 36.

Gallery of Quilts

Oregon Garden, 46" x 23"

Hydrangeas in the Summer, 23" x 31"

Garden Appliqué, 21" x 21"

Notice that the appliqués are attached with Velcro.
When removed, they reveal hidden surprises.

Christening Day, 16" x 14"

Sunflower Girl, 16" x 10"

By the Sea, 37" x 16"

Resources

Bubble Jet Set
www.cjenkinscompany.com

Color Textiles
9030 West Sahara, #198
Las Vegas, NV 89117
612-382-0013
www.colortextiles.com

The Electric Quilt Company
419 Gould Street, Suite 2
Bowling Green, OH 43402-3047
800-356-4219
www.electricquilt.com

Epson
www.epson.com

Fotolia
www.fotolia.com

Frankie's Fabric Photo Printing
440-265-9321
www.fabricphotoprinting.com

Hewlett-Packard Company
www.hp.com

Joe Hesch Enterprises
www.joehesch.com

June Tailor
PO Box 208
2861 Highway 175
Richfield, WI 53076
800-844-5400
www.junetailor.com

Kaleidoscope Kreator
www.kaleidoscopecollections.com

Poster 7
www.poster7.com

Printed Treasures
www.printedtreasures.com

The Vintage Workshop, LLC
PO Box 30237
Kansas City, MO 64112
913-341-5559
www.thevintageworkshop.com

CANBY PUBLIC LIBRARY
292 N. HOLLY
CANBY, OR 97013

About the Authors

Joe Hesch

Joe has been working in the field of marketing, education, and communication for over 20 years. A native Minnesotan, Joe has a BS in management/communication and an MBA with a minor in marketing from Concordia University in Oregon. As the owner of Joe Hesch Enterprises, he helps manufacturers and retailers learn technology and increase sales with marketing strategies and education techniques. As the former quilting and scrapbooking education manager at Hewlett Packard, Joe spent his time developing new ways to use technology in the sewing and quilting industries. Joe has appeared on over 100 national television programs, such as the popular series *America Quilts Creatively* and *America Sews with Sue Hausmann*. Joe was the technical director on two other books, *Photo Fun* and *More Photo Fun*, about fabric printing and quilting.

Whether it is through articles, classes, or one-on-one training, Joe enjoys helping people discover just how easy it is to incorporate the use of computers, cameras, and printers into their craft. Joe brings his hands-on approach to every class he teaches at colleges, trade shows, and retail stores.

Frankie Seme

Inspired by her home economics teacher to design and create her own prom dress at age 16, Frankie discovered her love for sewing. Frankie pursued this passion by attending the Virginia Marti College of Art and Design in Lakewood, Ohio, where she majored in fashion design. While attending Virginia Marti, Frankie began to develop her career doing custom bridal design. This business grew into a successful retail operation over the last 11 years and is now known as Frankie's Fabric Photo Printing. Frankie has been featured in the *Plain Dealer* newspaper in Cleveland and in the *Royalton Recorder* for her sewing skills, design expertise, and bridal-gown knowledge. Over the years, Frankie has taught beginner sewing classes, serger classes, and advanced sewing classes for JoAnn Fabrics as well as for her own retail business. Frankie continues to teach embroidery programs, technology events, creative quilting classes, and sewing for all ages. You can see some of Frankie's projects published in VDTA magazine, *Pfaff Creative Magazine*, and in the 2003 *Better Homes and Gardens Sewing* publication, as well as on the *Sew Young Sew Fun* and *Pfaff USA* Web sites.